ETHICAL HACKING AND CYBER-SECURITY

A Comprehensive Guide

Olanrewaju Sanni

This book is dedicated to God Almighty, the epitome of all wisdom and strength.

CONTENTS

INTRODUCTION

In today's digital age, where technology plays a paramount role in our lives, the importance of ethical hacking and cybersecurity has become more crucial than ever before. With the increasing reliance on interconnected systems and the rise of cyber threats, individuals and organizations need to be equipped with the necessary knowledge and skills to protect their data and networks from malicious attacks.

This book/course aims to provide a comprehensive understanding of ethical hacking principles, techniques, and cybersecurity best practices. By delving into the world of ethical hacking, learners will not only gain insights into how hackers exploit vulnerabilities but also learn how to proactively secure systems, networks, and data.

The objectives of this book/course revolve around building a strong foundation in ethical hacking and cybersecurity. Through a step-by-step approach, learners will be introduced to the fundamental concepts, tools, and methodologies used in ethical hacking. This includes understanding different attack vectors, learning about reconnaissance techniques, exploiting vulnerabilities, and securing systems against potential threats.

Furthermore, this book/course emphasizes the importance of ethical hacking and responsible use of hacking techniques. Ethical hackers play a critical role in identifying vulnerabilities and strengthening security measures to protect sensitive information. By equipping learners with the knowledge of ethical hacking, they can contribute to creating a safer digital environment while also gaining potential career opportunities in the cybersecurity field.

Throughout the book/course, practical examples, real-world scenarios, and hands-on exercises will be provided to enhance understanding and application of the concepts learned. Additionally, discussions on cybersecurity best practices, legal and ethical considerations, and emerging trends will further broaden the learner's perspective and ensure they are prepared to navigate the complex landscape of cybersecurity.

By the end of this book/course, learners will possess the necessary skills and knowledge to identify potential vulnerabilities, protect against common cyber threats, and implement effective security measures. Whether you are an aspiring ethical hacker, IT professional, or someone who wishes to enhance their understanding of cybersecurity, this book/course serves as a valuable resource in establishing a solid foundation in ethical hacking principles and cybersecurity best practices.

CHAPTER 1: INTRODUCTION TO ETHICAL HACKING

Section 1: Understanding the role of an ethical hacker and their responsibilities.

Introduction:

In this chapter, we will delve into the world of ethical hacking and explore the various aspects that make it an essential practice in today's cybersecurity landscape. We will begin by understanding the role of an ethical hacker and the responsibilities they carry.

1.1 Defining Ethical Hacking:

Ethical hacking, also referred to as white-hat hacking or penetration testing, involves the authorized and legal assessment of computer systems, networks, and applications to identify vulnerabilities. Ethical hackers assume the role of a malicious attacker to detect weaknesses before they can be exploited by real threats.

1.2 The Need for Ethical Hackers:

With the rapid advancement of technology and the increasing number of cyber threats, organizations require skilled professionals who can simulate and anticipate potential attacks. Ethical hackers play a critical role in identifying security flaws and fortifying system defenses, helping organizations safeguard their sensitive information.

1.3 Responsibilities of an Ethical Hacker:

Ethical hackers operate within a framework of responsibilities that differentiate them from malicious hackers. Their main objectives include:

a) Obtaining proper authorization: Ethical hackers must obtain explicit permission from the owner of the system before initiating any hacking attempts. This ensures that their actions are legal and ethical.

b) Conducting thorough assessments: Ethical hackers employ various techniques to identify vulnerabilities in systems, networks, and applications. They utilize their skills and knowledge to detect weaknesses that could potentially be exploited by malicious actors.

c) Providing comprehensive reports: After completing an assessment, ethical hackers compile detailed reports highlighting the vulnerabilities they discovered, along with recommendations for mitigating those risks. These reports serve as valuable resources for organizations to improve their security posture.

d) Continuous learning and professional development: Ethical hackers must stay updated with the latest trends, techniques, and tools in cybersecurity. This ongoing learning process enables them to effectively adapt to emerging threats and ensure they remain proficient in their craft.

Section 2: Exploring the legal and ethical aspects of ethical hacking.

2.1 Ethical Considerations:

Ethical hackers hold themselves accountable to high standards of ethics while conducting their activities. Some key ethical considerations include:

a) Respect for privacy: Ethical hackers must respect the privacy rights of individuals and organizations. They should refrain from accessing or compromising personal data unless explicitly authorized to do so.

b) Avoiding unnecessary harm: Ethical hackers need to ensure that their actions do not cause harm or disruption to systems, networks, or services during their assessments.

c) Abiding by legal requirements: Ethical hackers must comply with the laws and regulations governing cybersecurity practices in their jurisdiction. This includes obtaining proper consent, protecting user data, and adhering to disclosure guidelines.

2.2 Legal Implications:

Different countries have specific laws and regulations in place to regulate cybersecurity practices. Ethical hackers must familiarize themselves with the legal environment and ensure their work aligns with these requirements. Some legal aspects to consider include:

a) Authorization and consent: Ethical hackers must obtain explicit authorization to conduct their assessments, ensuring that they have the legal right to engage in hacking activities within defined boundaries.

b) Data protection and confidentiality: Ethical hackers must handle any sensitive data they come across during their assessments with utmost care. Complying with data protection laws and maintaining confidentiality is crucial.

Section 3: Overview of relevant laws and regulations.

3.1 International Laws and Frameworks:

There are various international laws, frameworks, and industry standards that provide guidance to ethical hackers. Some prominent examples include:

a) General Data Protection Regulation (GDPR): Enforced by the European Union, GDPR mandates the protection of personal data and imposes rules on how organizations handle such information.

b) Computer Fraud and Abuse Act (CFAA): In the United States, the CFAA defines and criminalizes unauthorized access to computer systems, emphasizing the importance of obtaining proper authorization.

c) ISO 27001: This internationally recognized standard outlines the best practices for establishing, implementing, maintaining, and continuously improving an Information Security Management System (ISMS).

Conclusion:

In this chapter, we have explored the role of an ethical hacker and the responsibilities they bear. We have also discussed the ethical considerations and legal implications associated with ethical hacking, along with an overview of relevant laws and regulations. Understanding these foundational principles is crucial for ethical hackers to navigate their roles effectively and ensure their actions align with legal requirements and ethical guidelines.

CHAPTER 2:
FUNDAMENTALS OF CYBERSECURITY

Section 1: Defining cybersecurity and its significance in protecting data and systems.

Introduction:

In this chapter, we will explore the fundamentals of cybersecurity and understand its significance in safeguarding data and systems from potential threats. We will begin by defining cybersecurity and highlighting its importance in today's interconnected world.

1.1 Understanding Cybersecurity:

Cybersecurity encompasses a set of practices, technologies, and measures designed to protect electronic systems, networks, and data from unauthorized access, damage, or theft. It involves the implementation of strategies that ensure the confidentiality, integrity, and availability of information in the digital realm.

1.2 The Significance of Cybersecurity:

The increasing reliance on digital technologies and interconnected systems has made cybersecurity a critical aspect of our daily lives. It plays a vital role in safeguarding sensitive information, preserving privacy, and maintaining the smooth functioning of organizations and individuals alike. By protecting against cyber threats, cybersecurity helps build trust, enhances resilience, and prevents potentially devastating consequences.

Section 2: Overview of different types of cyber threats, vulnerabilities, and attack vectors.

2.1 Types of Cyber Threats:

Cyber threats can take various forms, each with its unique characteristics and potential impact. Some common types of cyber threats include:

a) Malware: Malicious software, such as viruses, worms, and ransomware, is designed to exploit vulnerabilities and compromise systems or data.

b) Phishing: Phishing attacks aim to trick individuals

into revealing sensitive information, such as passwords or credit card details, by masquerading as trustworthy entities through emails, messages, or websites.

c) Denial of Service (DoS) Attacks: These attacks flood systems or networks with excessive traffic, rendering them unable to respond to legitimate requests.

d) Social Engineering: Social engineering manipulates human psychology to deceive individuals into disclosing confidential information or granting unauthorized access.

2.2 Vulnerabilities and Attack Vectors:

Vulnerabilities are weaknesses or flaws in systems, networks, or applications that can be exploited by threat actors. Attack vectors are the means by which attackers gain access to these vulnerabilities. Some common vulnerabilities and attack vectors include:

a) Software vulnerabilities: Flaws in software code, including programming errors or misconfigurations, can create entry points for attacks.

b) Weak authentication: Inadequate password policies or weak authentication mechanisms can allow unauthorized access to systems or accounts.

c) Insider threats: Employees or individuals with authorized access may abuse their privileges or unintentionally compromise security.

d) Network vulnerabilities: Poorly configured networks, insecure protocols, or outdated hardware can provide opportunities for attackers to gain unauthorized access.

Section 3: Introduction to common security frameworks and standards.

3.1 Security Frameworks:

To establish effective cybersecurity practices, organizations often adopt various security frameworks that provide guidelines and best practices. Some popular security frameworks include:

a) NIST Cybersecurity Framework: Developed by the National Institute of Standards and Technology (NIST), this framework provides a flexible approach to cybersecurity risk management, focusing on asset protection, threat detection, and incident response.

b) ISO 27001: This international standard outlines the requirements for establishing, implementing, maintaining, and continually improving an Information Security Management System (ISMS).

c) CIS Controls: The Center for Internet Security (CIS) Controls offers a set of prioritized actions to protect organizations against prevalent cyber threats.

3.2 Security Standards:

In addition to frameworks, there are several established security standards that organizations can adhere to for ensuring robust cybersecurity practices. These standards include:

a) Payment Card Industry Data Security Standard (PCI DSS): Designed for organizations handling cardholder data, PCI DSS ensures the secure processing, storage, and transmission of payment card information.

b) Health Insurance Portability and Accountability Act (HIPAA): HIPAA establishes security and privacy requirements for protecting medical information and patient data.

c) General Data Protection Regulation (GDPR): Enforced by the European Union, GDPR specifies rules for handling personal data and imposes obligations on organizations that interact with EU citizens.

Conclusion:

In this chapter, we have explored the fundamentals of cybersecurity. We defined cybersecurity and emphasized its significance in protecting data and systems. Furthermore, we discussed different types of cyber threats, vulnerabilities, and attack vectors, which organizations need to be aware of to effectively counter potential risks. Finally, we introduced common security frameworks and standards that provide guidelines for establishing robust cybersecurity practices. Understanding these fundamentals sets the stage for implementing proactive measures to protect against cyber threats and ensure the integrity of sensitive information and systems.

CHAPTER 3: NETWORKING ESSENTIALS

Section 1: Understanding the basics of networking protocols, architectures, and devices.

Introduction:

In this chapter, we will delve into the fundamentals of networking. We will explore the different protocols, architectures, and devices that enable communication and data transfer within networks.

1.1 Networking Protocols:

Networking protocols are a set of rules and standards that govern how data is transmitted, received, and processed across networks. Some widely used protocols include:

a) Internet Protocol (IP): IP provides the addressing scheme and routing capabilities necessary for data to be delivered across interconnected networks.

b) Transmission Control Protocol (TCP): TCP ensures reliable and ordered delivery of data by providing error checking, flow control, and congestion control mechanisms.

c) Hypertext Transfer Protocol (HTTP): HTTP enables the retrieval and display of web pages and other resources over the internet.

1.2 Networking Architectures:

Networking architectures define the structure, components, and interactions within a network. Two common architectures are:

a) Client-Server Architecture: In this model, clients make requests to servers, which process those requests and send back the requested information or services.

b) Peer-to-Peer Architecture: In a peer-to-peer network, devices connect directly to each other without relying on a central server. Each device can act as both a client and a server.

1.3 Networking Devices:

Networking devices facilitate the transfer of data between devices within a network. Some essential networking devices include:

a) Routers: Routers direct and forward data packets between different networks, ensuring that they reach their intended destinations.

b) Switches: Switches create and manage communication channels within a network, allowing devices to send data directly to their intended recipients.

c) Firewalls: Firewalls monitor and control network traffic, enforcing security policies to protect against unauthorized access and malicious activities.

Section 2: Introduction to IP addressing, subnetting, and network topologies.

2.1 IP Addressing:

IP addressing is a fundamental aspect of networking that allows devices to communicate over a network. An IP address is a unique identifier assigned to each device connected to a network, enabling the exchange of data. IPv4 and IPv6 are two versions of the IP protocol, each with its own addressing scheme.

2.2 Subnetting:

Subnetting is the process of dividing a network into smaller subnetworks, called subnets. This technique allows efficient utilization of IP addresses and helps organize devices within a network based on their location or function.

2.3 Network Topologies:

Network topologies refer to the physical or logical layout of devices in a network. Common types of network topologies include:

a) Bus Topology: In a bus topology, devices are connected to a single communication line, called a bus. Data is transmitted through the bus and received by all devices on the network.

b) Star Topology: In a star topology, devices are connected to a central device, like a switch or hub, which controls the flow of data between devices.

c) Mesh Topology: In a mesh topology, devices are interconnected with several redundant paths, ensuring multiple routes for data transmission and improving network reliability.

Section 3: Exploring network security principles and defenses.

3.1 Network Security Principles:

Network security involves protecting networks and their associated devices from unauthorized access, data loss, and malicious activities. Some core principles of network security include:

a) Confidentiality: Ensuring that data is accessible only to authorized individuals or entities.

b) Integrity: Maintaining the accuracy and consistency of data by guarding against unauthorized modifications.

c) Availability: Ensuring that network resources and services are readily accessible when needed.

3.2 Network Security Defenses:

To safeguard networks, various security defenses are employed. These defenses include:

a) Access Control: Implementing measures such as

strong authentication, authorization, and accounting (AAA) to control who can access the network.

b) Intrusion Detection and Prevention Systems: These systems detect and prevent unauthorized access attempts or malicious activities within the network.

c) Encryption: Encrypting data in transit or at rest to protect it from unauthorized interception or tampering.

Conclusion:

In this chapter, we explored the essentials of networking. We learned about networking protocols, architectures, and devices that facilitate communication and data transfer within networks. We also discussed IP addressing, subnetting, and different network topologies. Lastly, we explored network security principles and defenses that are crucial for ensuring the confidentiality, integrity, and availability of network resources. By understanding these networking fundamentals, you are well-equipped to build and secure robust networks that meet the needs of modern digital environments.

CHAPTER 4:
RECONNAISSANCE AND FOOTPRINTING

Section 1: Overview of information gathering techniques to assess target systems.

Introduction:

Reconnaissance and footprinting are critical steps in the process of assessing target systems for potential vulnerabilities and weaknesses. In this chapter, we will explore various techniques used to gather information about target systems, including open-source intelligence (OSINT) and network scanning.

1.1 Information Gathering Techniques:

Information gathering involves collecting data about target systems, networks, and their associated entities. Some commonly used techniques include:

a) Passive information gathering: Passive techniques

involve gathering information without directly interacting with the target. This includes reviewing websites, analyzing DNS records, and monitoring social media.

b) Active information gathering: Active techniques involve actively probing the target systems or networks to gather information. This can include port scanning, email harvesting, or performing Whois queries.

Section 2: Introduction to footprinting, enumeration, and vulnerability scanning.

2.1 Footprinting:

Footprinting is the process of collecting information about a target system with the goal of creating a blueprint or "footprint" of its infrastructure. Footprinting techniques include:

a) DNS footprinting: Gathering information about the domain name system (DNS) infrastructure associated with the target system, such as IP addresses and mail servers.

b) Network footprinting: Identifying the network infrastructure of the target system, including routers, switches, and firewalls.

2.2 Enumeration:

Enumeration involves actively probing a target system to discover information about its structure, user accounts, and services. Enumeration techniques include:

a) Port scanning: Scanning for open ports on the target system to identify running services and potential entry points.

b) Service enumeration: Gathering information about the specific services running on the target system, such as HTTP, FTP, or SSH.

2.3 Vulnerability scanning:

Vulnerability scanning involves assessing the target system for known vulnerabilities and weaknesses. This is done by using specialized tools that scan the system for security holes and misconfigurations. The results of vulnerability scans can help prioritize efforts for further exploitation.

Section 3: Exploiting open-source intelligence (OSINT) for reconnaissance.

3.1 Understanding OSINT:

Open-source intelligence (OSINT) refers to information that is publicly available and can be collected from various sources, such as websites, social media, online forums, and public databases. OSINT provides valuable insights into target systems and organizations.

3.2 Using OSINT for reconnaissance:

OSINT can be leveraged during the reconnaissance phase to gather information such as:

a) Company details: Collecting information about the target organization, including its structure, key personnel, and business partners.

b) Social engineering opportunities: Identifying potential points of weakness within an organization's workforce by analyzing employee profiles and interactions.

c) Infrastructure details: Gathering information about the target system's IP addresses, domain names, and associated network infrastructure.

Conclusion:

In this chapter, we explored the crucial steps of reconnaissance and footprinting. We discussed information gathering techniques for assessing target systems, including passive and active methods. We also introduced footprinting, enumeration, and vulnerability scanning as essential steps in understanding target systems' infrastructure and potential vulnerabilities. Lastly, we covered open-source intelligence (OSINT) and its significance in reconnaissance, enabling us to gather valuable information from publicly available sources. By employing these techniques, you will be able to gather detailed insights and effectively assess target systems for potential security risks.

CHAPTER 5: SCANNING AND ENUMERATION

Section 1: Analyzing network scanning techniques and port scanning methodologies.

Introduction:

Network scanning and port scanning are essential steps in the process of identifying potential vulnerabilities and weaknesses within target systems. In this chapter, we will delve into various scanning techniques used to analyze networks and methodologies employed for port scanning.

1.1 Network Scanning Techniques:

Network scanning involves examining a target network to discover active hosts, open ports, and services. Some commonly used network scanning techniques include:

a) Ping sweep: This technique involves sending ICMP Echo Request (ping) packets to a range of IP addresses to determine which hosts are online.

b) ARP scanning: By sending Address Resolution Protocol (ARP) requests to a network, it is possible to determine the IP-to-MAC address mapping of hosts in the network.

c) TCP connect scanning: This method involves initiating full TCP handshakes with target systems to determine which ports are open or closed.

1.2 Port Scanning Methodologies:

Port scanning is the process of sending messages to target systems' ports to identify open ports and services. Different methodologies for port scanning include:

a) TCP scanning: This technique involves sending TCP packets to specific ports on target systems to determine their status (open, closed, or filtered).

b) UDP scanning: UDP scanning involves sending UDP packets to target systems to identify open or closed ports that respond to UDP datagrams.

c) SYN scanning: SYN scanning leverages the TCP three-way handshake process to identify open ports by analyzing the server's response to SYN packets.

Section 2: Identifying open ports, services, and vulnerabilities.

2.1 Identifying Open Ports:

Open ports are crucial entry points that allow communication with services running on target systems. By identifying open ports, potential vulnerabilities can be discovered. Techniques for identifying open ports include:

a) TCP and UDP port scanning: Using the port scanning methodologies mentioned earlier, open ports can be identified by analyzing the responses received from the target systems.

b) Banner grabbing: This technique involves capturing information from service banners (responses) received from open ports to determine the services running on those ports.

2.2 Identifying Services and Vulnerabilities:

Once open ports are identified, the next step is to determine the services running on those ports and search for potential vulnerabilities. Techniques for identifying services and vulnerabilities include:

a) Service identification: By analyzing the responses received from open ports (banner grabbing), information about the specific services running on those ports can be obtained.

b) Vulnerability scanning: Utilizing specialized tools, vulnerability scans can be conducted to identify known vulnerabilities associated with the services running on open ports.

Section 3: Conducting enumeration to gather detailed system information.

3.1 Enumeration Process:

Enumeration involves gathering detailed system information by actively probing and querying target systems. The goal is to gather information such as user accounts, shared resources, and configuration details. Techniques used for enumeration include:

a) NetBIOS and SNMP enumeration: Leveraging protocols like NetBIOS and Simple Network Management Protocol (SNMP) to extract information about the target system's users, shares, and configuration.

b) LDAP and DNS enumeration: Querying Lightweight Directory Access Protocol (LDAP) servers and Domain Name System (DNS) servers to gather information about users, groups, and network infrastructure.

Conclusion:

In this chapter, we explored the fundamental aspects of scanning and enumeration in the context of assessing target systems. We examined network scanning techniques to identify active hosts, and port scanning methodologies to discover open ports and services. By utilizing these methods, we can gain valuable insights into potential vulnerabilities within target systems. Additionally, we discussed techniques for identifying open ports, services, and conducting vulnerability scans. Finally, we explored the process of enumeration, which allows us to gather detailed system information through active probing and querying. By utilizing these techniques effectively, you will be able to conduct thorough assessments and strengthen the security of target systems.

CHAPTER 6: SYSTEM HACKING

Section 1: Exploring techniques for bypassing system security controls.

Introduction:

System hacking involves bypassing security controls to gain unauthorized access, escalate privileges, and move laterally within a target system. In this chapter, we will dive into various techniques used to compromise system security controls and explore ways to mitigate these risks.

1.1 Exploiting Vulnerabilities:

Exploiting vulnerabilities is a common technique used by attackers to gain unauthorized access to systems. Vulnerability identification and exploitation involve the following steps:

a) Vulnerability scanning: Discovering weaknesses and security flaws in target systems using automated scanners or manual assessment techniques.

b) Exploit development: Creating or utilizing existing exploits to take advantage of identified vulnerabilities and gain unauthorized access.

c) Remote code execution: Leveraging discovered vulnerabilities to execute malicious code remotely, providing unauthorized access to the system.

1.2 Social Engineering:

Social engineering is a technique that targets human psychology to manipulate individuals into revealing sensitive information or granting unauthorized access. Common social engineering techniques include:

a) Phishing: Sending deceptive emails or messages to trick users into revealing passwords, personal information, or installing malware.

b) Pretexting: Creating a false scenario or identity to gain the trust of individuals and extract sensitive information from them.

c) Impersonation: Posing as a trusted individual or authority figure to deceive targets and obtain confidential information or gain system access.

Section 2: Gaining unauthorized access, privilege escalation, and lateral movement.

2.1 Unauthorized Access:

Unauthorized access refers to gaining entry into a system or network without proper authorization. Techniques for gaining unauthorized access include:

a) Password cracking: Utilizing software tools or methods to decrypt passwords or guess weak credentials.

b) Exploiting misconfigurations: Identifying misconfigured services, applications, or systems that can be abused to gain unauthorized access.

c) Brute-force attacks: Trying all possible combinations of login credentials to gain access by systematically guessing passwords.

2.2 Privilege Escalation:

Privilege escalation involves obtaining higher-level access privileges within a system or network. Techniques for privilege escalation include:

a) Exploiting software vulnerabilities: Exploiting software flaws or vulnerabilities to elevate user privileges and gain administrative access.

b) Misusing legitimate privileges: Exploiting excessive or misconfigured user permissions to elevate privileges and gain unauthorized access.

2.3 Lateral Movement:

Lateral movement is the process of moving horizontally within a compromised network or system to access other resources or systems. Techniques for lateral movement include:

a) Exploiting compromised credentials: Using stolen or compromised credentials to authenticate and access different systems within the network.

b) Pass-the-hash attacks: Leveraging hashed credentials obtained from one system to gain unauthorized access to other systems.

Section 3: Introduction to password cracking, keyloggers, and rootkits.

3.1 Password Cracking:

Password cracking is the process of recovering passwords from hashed values or guessing them using various methods. Techniques for password cracking include:

a) Brute-force attacks: Trying all possible combinations of characters until the correct password is found.

b) Dictionary attacks: Trying commonly used or previously leaked passwords from a predefined list.

3.2 Keyloggers:

Keyloggers are malicious programs designed to record keystrokes entered by users on a compromised system. They can be hardware or software-based. Keyloggers help attackers steal sensitive information like passwords, credit card details, etc., by intercepting keystrokes.

3.3 Rootkits:

Rootkits are stealthy malware designed to hide the

presence of malicious activities or processes in an infected system. Rootkits often involve modifying system files or components to gain persistent access and maintain control over compromised systems.

Conclusion:

In this chapter, we delved into the realm of system hacking, exploring techniques used to bypass security controls, gain unauthorized access, escalate privileges, and move laterally within target systems. We discussed vulnerability exploitation, social engineering, and methods for gaining unauthorized access. We also touched upon privilege escalation, lateral movement, and introduced password cracking, keyloggers, and rootkits. It is essential to understand these techniques to better protect systems and networks from potential attacks. Implementing strong security measures, such as regular patching, user awareness training, and multi-factor authentication, can help mitigate the risks associated with system hacking.

CHAPTER 7: WEB APPLICATION SECURITY

Section 1: Understanding common web application vulnerabilities.

Introduction:

Web applications play a critical role in today's digital landscape. However, they are often targeted by attackers due to their potential vulnerabilities. In this chapter, we will explore some of the most common web application vulnerabilities, understand how they can be exploited, and discuss ways to mitigate these risks.

1.1 SQL Injection:

SQL injection occurs when an attacker is able to manipulate a web application's database queries by inserting malicious SQL code. This can lead to unauthorized access to sensitive data or even complete control over the underlying database. Mitigating SQL injection vulnerabilities involves implementing proper input validation, parameterized queries, and least privilege principles.

1.2 Cross-Site Scripting (XSS):

Cross-Site Scripting involves injecting malicious scripts into web pages viewed by other users. This vulnerability allows attackers to steal sensitive information, hijack user sessions, or deface websites. Preventative measures for XSS vulnerabilities include input sanitization, output encoding, and implementing Content Security Policies (CSP) to restrict the execution of untrusted scripts.

1.3 Cross-Site Request Forgery (CSRF):

CSRF attacks exploit the trust between a user's browser and a web application. By tricking a user into performing an unintended action, an attacker can carry out actions on behalf of the user without their consent. Preventing CSRF vulnerabilities involves implementing anti-CSRF tokens, validating referrer headers, and utilizing Same-Site cookies.

Section 2: Introduction to web application penetration testing methodologies.

2.1 Penetration Testing:

Penetration testing, also known as ethical hacking, involves assessing the security of web applications by simulating real-world attacks. It helps identify vulnerabilities and provides recommendations for remediation. A typical web application penetration test follows the following steps:

a) Reconnaissance: Gathering information about the target application, including its architecture, technologies used, and potential attack vectors.

b) Vulnerability scanning: Identifying common web application vulnerabilities using automated tools or manual techniques.

c) Exploitation: Attempting to exploit identified vulnerabilities to gain unauthorized access or perform malicious actions.

d) Post-exploitation: Assessing the impact of successful exploitation and providing recommendations for remediation.

2.2 OWASP Testing Guide:

The Open Web Application Security Project (OWASP) provides a comprehensive guide for conducting web application security testing. The OWASP Testing Guide includes various testing methodologies, tools, and techniques to evaluate the security posture of web applications. It covers areas like authentication, session management, input validation, and secure configuration.

Section 3: Overview of secure coding practices.

3.1 Secure Development Lifecycle (SDL):

Implementing secure coding practices is crucial for building resilient web applications. The Secure Development Lifecycle involves integrating security considerations into every phase of application development, including requirements gathering, design, implementation, testing, and deployment. Following secure coding practices helps prevent common vulnerabilities, such as injection attacks, insecure direct object references, and insecure deserialization.

3.2 Input Validation and Output Encoding:

Web applications should validate and sanitize all user inputs to prevent injection attacks and other vulnerabilities. Output encoding ensures that user-supplied data is properly encoded before displaying it back to users, thus preventing XSS attacks.

3.3 Least Privilege Principle:

Adhering to the least privilege principle ensures that web applications operate with the minimum privileges necessary to perform their intended functions. This minimizes the potential impact of any vulnerabilities that may be exploited.

Conclusion:

Web application security is vital to protect sensitive data and maintain the trust of users. Understanding common vulnerabilities like SQL injection, XSS, and CSRF is essential for developers and security professionals. Conducting regular web application penetration tests helps identify weaknesses and implement appropriate security measures. Additionally, following secure coding practices, such as input validation, output encoding, and adhering to the least privilege principle, contributes to building robust and resilient web applications. By prioritizing security throughout the development lifecycle, organizations can ensure the safety of their web applications and safeguard against potential threats.

CHAPTER 8: NETWORK SECURITY

Section 1: Exploring different network attacks and countermeasures.

Introduction:

Network security is crucial in safeguarding the integrity, confidentiality, and availability of data transmitted over networks. In this chapter, we will explore various network attacks, understand how they can be mitigated, and discuss countermeasures to enhance network security.

1.1 Denial of Service (DoS) Attacks:

Denial of Service attacks aim to disrupt the availability of a network or its resources by overwhelming them with a flood of illegitimate traffic. Countermeasures for DoS attacks include traffic filtering, rate limiting, and deploying redundant resources to handle increased load.

1.2 Man-in-the-Middle (MitM) Attacks:

MitM attacks involve intercepting and altering communication between two parties without their knowledge. Encryption mechanisms such as Secure Sockets Layer/Transport Layer Security (SSL/TLS) can protect against MitM attacks. Additionally, implementing strong authentication methods and monitoring network traffic can help detect and prevent such attacks.

1.3 Brute Force Attacks:

Brute force attacks involve systematically attempting all possible combinations of passwords or encryption keys until the correct one is found. Protecting against brute force attacks requires implementing account lockouts, strong password policies, and multi-factor authentication.

Section 2: Introduction to firewall, Intrusion Detection and Prevention Systems (IDS/IPS), and Virtual Private Networks (VPNs).

2.1 Firewalls:

Firewalls serve as the first line of defense in network security. They monitor and control incoming and outgoing network traffic based on predefined security rules. Firewalls can be implemented as hardware appliances or software applications, providing protection against unauthorized access, network-based attacks, and malware.

2.2 Intrusion Detection and Prevention Systems (IDS/IPS):

IDS/IPS systems detect and prevent network-based attacks and intrusions. IDS monitors network traffic, identifies suspicious patterns or events, and raises alerts. IPS goes a step further and actively blocks or mitigates detected threats. Implementing IDS/IPS aids in real-time threat identification, alerting, and proactive network protection.

2.3 Virtual Private Networks (VPNs):

VPNs create secure, encrypted connections over an untrusted network, typically the internet. By using tunneling protocols and encryption algorithms, VPNs ensure that data transmitted between endpoints remains confidential and secure. VPNs allow remote employees to connect securely to corporate networks, protecting sensitive information from interception.

Section 3: Implementing network security controls.

3.1 Access Control:

Access control mechanisms ensure that only authorized individuals or devices can access a network or its resources. This includes implementing strong authentication methods like passwords or biometrics, role-based access controls, and regular user access reviews.

3.2 Network Segmentation:

Network segmentation involves dividing a network into smaller, isolated segments to reduce the impact of potential breaches. By separating critical assets from less sensitive ones, network segmentation helps contain threats and limit lateral movement within a network.

3.3 Patch Management:

Regularly updating software and firmware is essential to address vulnerabilities and protect against known exploits. Implementing a robust patch management process ensures that network devices and applications are up to date, reducing the risk of successful attacks.

Conclusion:

Network security is a multidimensional approach aimed at protecting the confidentiality, integrity, and availability of data transmitted over networks. Understanding different network attacks, such as DoS, MitM, and brute force attacks, enables organizations to implement effective countermeasures. Firewall, IDS/IPS, and VPN technologies provide essential layers of defense in securing network environments. Additionally, implementing access control mechanisms, network segmentation, and performing regular patch management aids in maintaining a secure network infrastructure. By prioritizing network security controls and staying vigilant against emerging threats, organizations can establish a robust network security posture and ensure the safety of their valuable data.

CHAPTER 9: INCIDENT RESPONSE AND HANDLING

Section 1: Understanding the incident response life cycle.

Introduction:

In today's digital landscape, incidents such as security breaches, data leaks, or network compromises are unfortunately common. This chapter focuses on understanding the incident response life cycle, developing an incident response plan, and conducting effective forensic investigations to mitigate and handle incidents.

1.1 Incident Response Life Cycle:

The incident response life cycle consists of six phases:

1. Preparation: Establishing an incident response team, defining roles and responsibilities, and creating an incident response plan.

2. Identification: Detecting and identifying potential security incidents through various monitoring and detection tools.

3. Containment: Isolating and containing the affected systems or networks to prevent further damage or spread of the incident.

4. Eradication: Removing the root cause of the incident, eliminating any malicious code, and restoring affected systems to a secure state.

5. Recovery: Restoring normal operations, verifying system integrity, and implementing measures to prevent similar incidents in the future.

6. Lessons Learned: Analyzing the incident, identifying weaknesses or gaps, and implementing improvements to the incident response plan and overall security posture.

Section 2: Developing an incident response plan and procedures.

2.1 Incident Response Plan:

An incident response plan outlines the framework for effectively handling and responding to incidents. It should include clear guidelines, roles and responsibilities, communication procedures, escalation paths, and steps for each phase of the incident response life cycle.

2.2 Incident Response Procedures:

Procedures provide step-by-step instructions for incident response actions, including how to identify, analyze, contain, eradicate, recover, and document incidents. They should cover technical and non-technical aspects, ensuring a consistent and coordinated response from the incident response team.

Section 3: Conducting forensic investigations and evidence handling.

3.1 Forensic Investigations:

Forensic investigations involve the collection, analysis, and preservation of digital evidence related to incidents. Trained forensic analysts use specialized tools and techniques to reconstruct events, identify the extent of the incident, and gather evidence for legal proceedings, if necessary.

3.2 Evidence Handling:

Proper evidence handling is crucial to maintain the integrity and admissibility of digital evidence. This includes documenting the chain of custody, employing forensic imaging, securing evidence in tamper-evident containers, and following relevant legal and regulatory guidelines.

Conclusion:

Incident response and handling is a critical aspect of maintaining a robust cybersecurity posture. Understanding the incident response life cycle helps organizations respond promptly and effectively to security incidents. Developing an incident response plan and procedures provides guidance for incident response teams, ensuring a coordinated and consistent approach. Additionally, conducting forensic investigations using proper evidence handling techniques allows organizations to gather evidence for analysis, remediation, and legal purposes if required. By continuously improving incident response capabilities, organizations can enhance their ability to detect, respond to, and recover from security incidents, minimizing the impact on their operations and protecting their valuable assets.

CHAPTER 10: THREAT INTELLIGENCE AND VULNERABILITY MANAGEMENT

Section 1: Introduction to threat intelligence and its role in proactive defense.

1.1 Understanding Threat Intelligence:

Threat intelligence is the process of collecting, analyzing, and interpreting information about potential and current threats to an organization's digital assets. It provides valuable insights into threat actors, their tactics, techniques, and procedures (TTPs), and emerging vulnerabilities. Effective threat intelligence allows organizations to proactively defend against cyber threats.

1.2 Role of Threat Intelligence in Proactive Defense:

Threat intelligence enables organizations to identify and understand potential threats, assess their relevance, and prioritize resources for effective defense. It helps in identifying vulnerabilities, tracking threat actors and their activities, sharing information with industry peers, and improving incident response capabilities. By leveraging threat intelligence, organizations can take proactive measures to prevent, detect, and respond to threats before they cause significant damage.

Section 2: Strategies for managing vulnerabilities and conducting vulnerability assessments.

2.1 Managing Vulnerabilities:

Managing vulnerabilities involves identifying, assessing, prioritizing, and remediating vulnerabilities within an organization's systems and networks. This is crucial to prevent cyber attacks that exploit weaknesses in software or configurations.

2.2 Vulnerability Assessments:

Vulnerability assessments involve systematically scanning and evaluating systems, networks, and applications to identify potential vulnerabilities. This includes both automated and manual assessments, leveraging tools and techniques to identify weaknesses and misconfigurations.

Section 3: Patch management and secure configuration strategies.

3.1 Patch Management:

Patch management refers to the process of identifying, testing, deploying, and monitoring software patches and updates. It is crucial for addressing known vulnerabilities and ensuring that systems and software are up to date with the latest security patches. Effective patch management helps mitigate the risk of exploitation by threat actors.

3.2 Secure Configuration Strategies:

Secure configuration strategies focus on implementing and maintaining secure settings for hardware, software, and network devices. This involves following industry best practices, hardening systems and applications, disabling unnecessary services, enforcing strong passwords, and implementing access controls. Secure configurations help reduce the attack surface and make it more difficult for threat actors to exploit vulnerabilities.

Conclusion:

Threat intelligence and vulnerability management are essential components of a proactive cybersecurity approach. By leveraging threat intelligence, organizations gain valuable insights into emerging threats, enabling them to take proactive defensive measures. Effective vulnerability management ensures that vulnerabilities are identified, prioritized, and remediated in a timely manner, reducing the risk of exploitation. Additionally, employing robust patch management and secure configuration strategies helps maintain the security posture of systems and networks. By combining these practices, organizations can enhance their ability to detect, prevent, and respond to emerging threats, minimizing the likelihood and impact of cyber attacks.

CHAPTER 11: SECURITY OPERATIONS AND MONITORING

Section 1: Overview of Security Operations Centers (SOCs) and security monitoring.

1.1 Understanding Security Operations Centers (SOCs):

A Security Operations Center (SOC) is a centralized unit within an organization responsible for monitoring, detecting, analyzing, and responding to security incidents. It serves as the nerve center for an organization's cybersecurity operations, working round-the-clock to defend against threats.

1.2 Importance of Security Monitoring:

Security monitoring involves the continuous monitoring of networks, systems, and applications to identify and respond to potential security incidents. It plays a critical role in early threat detection, enabling timely response and mitigation. Effective security monitoring provides organizations with the ability to proactively identify and address threats before they escalate.

Section 2: Implementing security controls for effective detection and response.

2.1 Security Controls for Detection and Response:

Implementing security controls is crucial for effectively detecting and responding to security incidents. These controls include network intrusion detection and prevention systems, advanced threat detection tools, endpoint protection solutions, and log management systems. By deploying these controls, organizations can strengthen their defense mechanisms, enabling efficient threat detection and response.

2.2 Security Information and Event Management (SIEM):

SIEM systems collect, correlate, and analyze event log data from various sources to detect and respond to security incidents. They provide real-time visibility into security events across the organization's IT infrastructure, enabling security teams to monitor and investigate suspicious activities. SIEM systems play a vital role in incident detection and response.

Section 3: Incident logging, analysis, and reporting.

3.1 Incident Logging:

Incident logging involves capturing and documenting relevant information about security incidents. This includes details such as the date and time of the incident, affected systems, incident description, and actions taken to mitigate the incident. Accurate and comprehensive incident logging helps in understanding the incident landscape, identifying trends, and improving incident response processes.

3.2 Incident Analysis:

Incident analysis involves examining collected data to understand the nature and impact of security incidents. It includes analyzing indicators of compromise (IOCs), conducting forensic investigations, and identifying the root causes of incidents. Incident analysis provides valuable insights into potential vulnerabilities, attack vectors, and the effectiveness of existing security controls.

3.3 Incident Reporting:

Incident reporting is the process of documenting and communicating the findings of incident analysis. It includes preparing reports that summarize the incident, its impact, response actions taken, and recommendations for preventing similar incidents in the future. Incident reports are essential for communication within the organization, sharing information with stakeholders, and facilitating improvements in security posture.

Conclusion:

Security operations and monitoring are vital components of a robust cybersecurity program. By establishing a Security Operations Center (SOC) and implementing effective security controls, organizations can proactively detect and respond to security incidents. Incident logging, analysis, and reporting are essential for understanding the threat landscape, identifying vulnerabilities, and improving incident response processes. By continually monitoring and analyzing security events, organizations can enhance their ability to detect, respond to, and mitigate potential threats, ensuring the protection of their digital assets.

CHAPTER 12: SECURITY AUDITING AND COMPLIANCE

Section 1: Exploring auditing methodologies and frameworks.

1.1 Auditing Methodologies:

Auditing methodologies provide structured approaches for evaluating the effectiveness of security controls, processes, and policies within an organization. Common methodologies include risk-based audits, control-based audits, and compliance-based audits. These methodologies help organizations identify gaps in their security posture and assess their overall risk exposure.

1.2 Auditing Frameworks:

Auditing frameworks provide guidelines and best practices for conducting security audits. Popular frameworks include the National Institute of Standards and Technology (NIST) Cybersecurity Framework, International Organization for Standardization (ISO)

27001, and Control Objectives for Information and Related Technologies (COBIT). These frameworks assist auditors in assessing and improving an organization's security program.

Section 2: Understanding compliance and regulatory requirements.

2.1 Compliance and Regulatory Requirements:

Compliance refers to adhering to specific laws, regulations, and industry standards relevant to an organization's operations. Examples of compliance requirements include the General Data Protection Regulation (GDPR) for protecting personal data, the Health Insurance Portability and Accountability Act (HIPAA) for safeguarding healthcare information, and the Payment Card Industry Data Security Standard (PCI DSS) for securing payment card data. Understanding these requirements is essential for organizations to avoid legal and financial consequences.

Section 3: Conducting security audits and assessments.

3.1 Security Audit Process:

The security audit process involves systematically examining an organization's security controls, policies, procedures, and systems to identify vulnerabilities, weaknesses, and non-compliance. It includes activities such as gathering evidence, testing controls, interviewing personnel, and reviewing documentation. The goal is to evaluate the effectiveness of security measures and identify areas that require improvement.

3.2 Vulnerability Assessments:

Vulnerability assessments are critical components of security audits. They involve identifying and assessing vulnerabilities within an organization's IT infrastructure, applications, and systems. Vulnerability scanning and penetration testing techniques are commonly used to uncover weaknesses and potential entry points for attackers. By conducting vulnerability assessments, organizations can proactively address vulnerabilities and enhance their security posture.

3.3 Compliance Audits:

Compliance audits focus on assessing an organization's adherence to specific legal and regulatory requirements. They involve evaluating whether the organization has implemented the necessary controls, policies, and procedures to comply with applicable regulations. Compliance audits help organizations identify gaps and ensure they meet the necessary standards to protect sensitive data and maintain regulatory compliance.

Conclusion:

Security auditing and compliance play crucial roles in maintaining a strong and secure cybersecurity posture. By following auditing methodologies and frameworks, organizations can effectively evaluate their security controls and procedures. Understanding compliance and regulatory requirements is vital to ensure adherence to legal obligations. Conducting regular security audits and assessments, including vulnerability assessments and compliance audits, enables organizations to identify weaknesses, address vulnerabilities, and improve their overall security and regulatory compliance.

SUMMARY

1. Throughout this book/course, we have covered a wide range of key concepts and techniques related to ethical hacking and cybersecurity. We have explored topics such as reconnaissance and enumeration, scanning and enumeration, system hacking, web application hacking, wireless network hacking, social engineering, and security auditing and compliance. By understanding these concepts and techniques, readers have gained valuable insights into how attackers exploit vulnerabilities and the measures needed to defend against them.

2. An underlying theme throughout this journey has been the importance of an ethical approach to hacking and the critical role of cybersecurity in safeguarding digital assets. Ethical hacking involves using hacking techniques for legitimate purposes, such as identifying vulnerabilities in systems and assisting organizations in enhancing their security posture. It is essential to emphasize that ethical hacking should only be conducted with proper authorization and within legal boundaries.

3. As technology continues to advance rapidly,

the field of ethical hacking and cybersecurity is constantly evolving. New threats and attack vectors emerge regularly, making it crucial for professionals in this field to continuously update their knowledge and skills. I encourage readers to remain curious, proactive, and committed to lifelong learning. Explore further resources, participate in training programs, attend conferences, and engage with the cybersecurity community to stay up to date with the latest trends and best practices.

By being vigilant and continuously improving their expertise, readers can make a significant impact in protecting digital assets, maintaining privacy, and ensuring the security of individuals, organizations, and society as a whole.

Remember, ethical hacking is a powerful tool for good when used responsibly and ethically. Let us remain dedicated to the pursuit of a secure and resilient digital world.

REFERENCES:

1. CEH (Certified Ethical Hacker) v11 Courseware. EC-Council. (2021).

2. Kim, S., & Solomon, D. (2019). Fundamentals of Information Systems Security. Jones & Bartlett Learning.

3. Peltier, T. R., & Peltier, J. B. (2020). Information Security Policies, Procedures, and Standards: A Practitioner's Reference. CRC Press.

4. Stamp, M. (2006). Information Security: Principles and Practice. John Wiley & Sons.

5. Whitman, M. E., & Mattord, H. J. (2019). Principles of Information Security. Cengage Learning.

6. Cheswick, W. R., Bellovin, S. M., & Rubin, A. D. (2003). Firewalls and Internet Security: Repelling the Wily Hacker. Addison-Wesley Professional.

7. Carroll, A., & Ostrowski, P. (2019). Cybersecurity: A Business Solution. CRC Press.

8. Eren, H., & Kılıç, V. (2020). Ethical Hacking and Penetration Testing Guide. Springer.

9. Mitnick, K. D., & Simon, W. L. (2002). The Art of Deception: Controlling the Human Element of Security. Wiley.

10. Bosworth, S., Kabay, M. E., & Whyne, E. (2011).

OLANREWAJU SANNI

Computer security handbook. Volume 2. John Wiley & Sons.

ABOUT THE AUTHOR

Olanrewaju Sanni

He is an educator and author. He studied Computer Science at Tai Solarin University of Education, Ijebu-Ode, Ogun State, Nigeria. He loves teaching computer studies and programming. He is married to his beautiful wife Tenny and God has blessed them with two children, Nehemiah and Pearl.